PHYSICAL SCIENCE

LIGHT

Please visit our web site at: **www.garethstevens.com**
For a free color catalog describing Gareth Stevens Publishing's list of high-quality books and multimedia programs, call 1-800-542-2595 (USA) or 1-800-387-3178 (Canada). Gareth Stevens Publishing's fax: (414) 332-3567.

Library of Congress Cataloging-in-Publication Data

Light.—North American ed.
        p. cm. — (Discovery Channel school science: physical science)
    Originally published: Shine. Bethesda, Md.: Discovery Enterprises, 2000.
    Summary: Explores the nature and properties of light, discussing such topics as refraction, the electromagnetic spectrum, optical illusions, and photons. Includes related activities.
    ISBN 0-8368-3359-7 (lib. bdg.)
    1. Light—Juvenile literature. [1. Light.] I. Title. II. Series.
QC360.S48 2003
535—dc21   2002030531

This edition first published in 2003 by
Gareth Stevens Publishing
A World Almanac Education Group Company
330 West Olive Street, Suite 100
Milwaukee, WI 53212 USA

This U.S. edition © 2003 by Gareth Stevens, Inc. First published in 2000 as *Shine: The Light Files* by Discovery Enterprises, LLC, Bethesda, Maryland. © 2000 by Discovery Communications, Inc.

Further resources for students and educators available at www.discoveryschool.com

Designed by Bill SMITH STUDIO
Project Editors: Justine Ciovacco, Lelia Mander, Sharon Yates, Anna Prokos
Designers: Nick Stone, Sonia Gauba, Bill Wilson, Darren D'Agostino, Joe Bartos, Dmitri Kushnirsky
Photo Editors: Jennifer Friel, Scott Haag
Art Buyers: Paula Radding, Marianne Tozzo
Gareth Stevens Editor: Betsy Rasmussen
Gareth Stevens Art Director: Tammy Gruenewald

Printed in the United States of America

1 2 3 4 5 6 7 8 9 07 06 05 04 03

Writers: Jackie Ball, Justine Ciovacco, Bill Doyle, Dan Franck, Lisa Krause, Susan Lewis, Diane Webber

Editor: Justine Ciovacco

Illustrations: p. 4, Stephen Wagner; p. 18, icons, Scott Mac Neil; p. 26, Lee MacLeod.

Photographs: Cover and pp. 2, 31, fiber optics, © Steve Allen/Image Bank; p. 3, eye © PhotoDisc; p. 3, globe, © MapArt; pp. 6–7, © PhotoDisc; p. 9, Antarctica, NASA; p. 9, Marie Curie © Archive Photos; p. 10, Huygen, CORBIS-Bettmann; p. 10, Newton, © LOC/Science Source; p. 10, Maxwell, Brown Brothers; p. 10, Foucault, © CORBIS-Bettmann; p. 11, Einstein stamp, U.S. Post Office; p. 11, Hertz,

Brown Brothers; p. 11, x-ray, © PhotoDisc; p. 11, fiber optics, © PhotoDisc; p. 12, Einstein, UPI/CORBIS-Bettmann; p. 12, pool, © PhotoDisc; pp. 14–15, © PhotoDisc; p. 16, Newton experiment, © Bettmann/CORBIS; p. 17, Newton's drawing, Smithsonian Museum; p. 18, #2/glory, © Galen Rowell/CORBIS; p. 18, mirage, © PhotoDisc; p. 19, face on mars, NASA; p. 24, Roentgen, Brown Brothers; p. 25, x-ray, © PhotoDisc; p. 26, laser in eye, Wolfgang Bayer/Discovery Communications, Inc.; pp. 26–27, Dr. Sylvia W. Norton; p. 28, guide dog, © Visuals Unlimited; p. 29, eye, © PhotoDisc; p. 31, boy, DCI/David Waitz.

Acknowledgments: pp. 24–25, excerpts from EYEWITNESS TO SCIENCE. © 1995 by John Carey. Reprinted by permission of Harvard University Press.

LiGHT

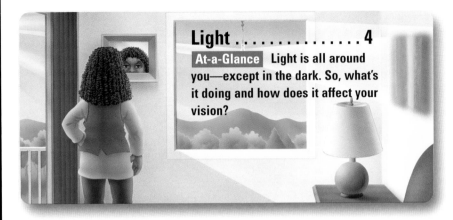

What's all around you and helps you to see, but you can't see it working? Light! As you read this, beams of white light are bouncing off the page and into your eyes. Working with your brain, your eyes are your guide to the lighted world around you. Or are they? Sometimes they trick you. But once you understand light, you might be able to make better sense out of everyday—and even extraordinary—sights.

In *LIGHT*, Discovery Channel tells the story of light—how we think about it, what it is, and how it affects our lives. What is truly striking is how something we take for granted every day lies at the very heart of our existence. Without light, there would be no world as we know it or as we see it. Of all nature's creations, light may be the most fundamental.

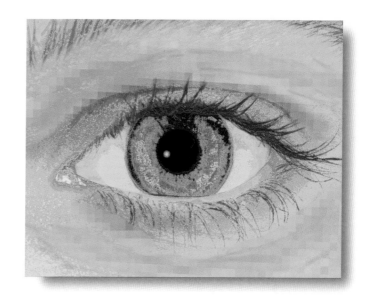

Who thought this produced light?
See page 10

Final Project

3

Light

Light streaming though an open window or brightening a room seems to be a common sight. And yet, our knowledge of light—what it is, and how it acts—has been the source of intense scientific interest since the beginning of human thought.

When you see a picture, you may be struck not by the science behind the light, but by its beauty: the way the light reflects or splits to make a rainbow of many colors. Light is a tool not just reserved for scientists. Painters, photographers, designers, writers, and even home decorators think about and use light's beauty and power in their work. This page shows you some of the phenomena associated with light.

That's interesting enough, but think about this: The speed of light through space is 186,000 miles (299,274 km) per second and nothing can go faster. This curious fact was one of the things that inspired Albert Einstein to develop his famous and very important Special Theory of Relativity. That's the idea that motion and time can only be measured in relation to the motion of the observer. Also, in the early 1900s, Einstein asked: What is light? Why can't anything go faster than it? Is light a wave, or a particle? Or is it both? Beyond light's commonness lie some of the deepest mysteries in all of science.

EYES—Animals have evolved structures that capture light, thus creating the ability to see the surrounding environment.

REFLECTION—Light is reflected off objects and sent back to our eyes.

SHADOW—Light can't reach all areas, so a blurry darker patch is what you see.

REFRACTION—Light is bent as it flows though one clear material to another, changing its direction. This can lead to some strange sights.

SPECTRUM—Light can be broken up into colored lights by a prism. Sunlight is known as white light. What are the colors in a rainbow?

ELECTRIC LIGHT—The Sun is not the only source of light. Can you think of others?

ABSORPTION—We see colored objects depending on how they absorb light. If an object completely absorbs all of the light, we see it as black. If it reflects all of the light, it's white. If an object absorbs all the colors in the spectrum except red, you see red.

You Light Up My Life

Q: Good morning and welcome to "Wake-Up Call," the sunrise show. You can't start your day without a wake-up call! And you can't start your morning without our special guest either. Isn't that right, Sunbeam?

A: That's right! Correct! Yessirree! No day begins without the sun rising and sending out gazillions of sunbeams, containing megajillions of light rays.

Q: You're sounding bright and full of energy today.

A: I'm ALWAYS bright! I have no choice. Sunbeams never turn off. We don't need plugs or batteries, either. And as for energy, I am *bursting* with energy! I have energy to burn because I come from the Big Bonfire in the sky—the Sun!

Matter of fact, how about you and me doing a few push-ups? I need to work some of this off.

Q: Uh, let's just talk, if you don't mind. Can you tell our viewers how long it took you to get here?

A: About 8 minutes, give or take a few seconds. Ninety-three million miles (150 million km) isn't that far when you're traveling at the speed of light. And there wasn't much traffic today. Just the usual clouds, vapors—the typical atmospheric stuff I always have to cut through. All in a day's work.

Q: Speaking of work, tell us more about your job. What's your average day like?

A: It's kind of fun. First of all, it's always a relief to be released from

that big blast furnace—6 million degrees at its core! We're talking HOT. But once I get to Earth, the fun really starts! I get one warm welcome!

Q: Why is that?

A: Because people love to see me coming, lighting up dark places, warming up cold places, spreading out the old solar energy, bouncing all over the place.

Q: What do you mean, bouncing?

A: Just what I said. Bouncing is the usual way light works to help you see an object. Another word for it is reflection. It's what happens when a ray of light hits a smooth surface like a mirror or a perfectly still pool of water.

Another ray bounces back at exactly the same angle and enters your eye. The image you see is reversed because of the way your eye and your brain work together.

Q: What if someone jumps into the pool and makes waves? Then what happens to the light?

A: Then the rays of light are scattered. They bounce back images that are messed up and confused. Hey, it's not *my* fault. I do my best. And anyway, bouncing isn't the only way light works. There's also bending, which is also known as refraction.

Q: How does that work?

A: Just like it sounds. Light gets bent, or curved, when it passes through something transparent, like glass. Bending can make objects look bigger because they widen the angle at which the rays enter your eyes.

Q: So is that how a magnifying glass works?

A: Sure is. And it's how reading glasses and contact lenses work too. Spread out that light! Pump up that image! Helps me do my job.

Q: Which is?

A: Bringing light to your eyes. They can't give out light on their own. They're just receivers for what I send their way. Supplying you with enough light is the true test of a ray of visible light.

Q: Visible light? You mean there's invisible light?

A: Of course. There are infrared and ultraviolet as well as visible light. We're all part of the electromagnetic spectrum—waves of energy that the Sun sends down. Pieces of the Sun itself. And every kind of electromagnetic wave has a different length. We're quite a group.

Q: I guess so. But do you ever wish you were invisible?

A: Nope. I like beaming down on everybody. And even though I'm visible, there's more to me than meets the eye.

Q: What do you mean?

A: Here's a little hint: What color am I?

Q: That's easy: bright white. Well, with maybe a tiny tinge of yellow.

A: Nope. You only *see* bright white. Sunlight actually contains red, orange, yellow, green, blue, and violet.

Q: But those are the colors in a rainbow!

A: Right. You see them in a rainbow because raindrops in the air bend and reflect sunlight and make the colors spread out and separate. You can bend sunlight into different colors yourself with a prism or a diamond or a crystal water glass. But you know, it's been great chatting, but I've got to go. Sun's been up for an hour and I have work to do. And energy to burn!

Activity

THE RELATIVITY OF RAYS Ultraviolet, or UV, light is the light wave that causes humans to sunburn. If you look on bottles of sunscreen lotions, you'll see that there are different "SPF" ratings. What does SPF mean? How are those numbers determined? Find out the answers to the questions either by researching or asking a pharmacist. When you get the answers, figure out which SPF is best for you and all of your family members—and let them know your findings.

BEYOND THE VISIBLE

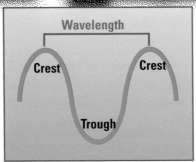

Wavelength

Crest   Crest

Trough

Invisible rays are bombarding you right now. They are everywhere, carrying radio and television signals, cellular phone conversations, and even warmth from the Sun. They are related to the light that is helping you read this page because they are all different wavelengths of electromagnetic radiation.

The Sun is the primary source of energy for Earth, arriving as light with a range of wavelengths. But the atmosphere absorbs many of the wavelengths before they reach us. Visible light waves come through, of course, and so do infrared waves—which you feel as heat. All of the wavelengths of the electromagnetic spectrum have found valuable uses in our lives.

The light that you see makes up just a small fraction of the total energy in light waves. We measure the waves in wavelengths, or the distance between a point on one wave to an identical point on the next wave (see diagram). Waves have many different lengths, but the shorter they are, the higher the energy they transmit. And regardless of the length, all electromagnetic waves race along at the same speed: 186,000 miles (299,274 km) per second, the speed of light.

The Electromagnetic Spectrum

Radio waves Radio waves range in length from several miles to about one foot. They carry television, cellular phone, and AM and FM radio signals. Radio telescopes "listen" for radio waves transmitted from distant galaxies and stars.

Microwaves Radio waves shorter than 11.8 inches (30 cm) are called microwaves. In microwave ovens, microwaves cause water molecules to bounce against each other and change places, cooking the food. Microwaves also power radar, which is used to track aircraft.

Infrared Warm objects, such as the Sun, give off heat that can be felt as infrared waves. Red-hot coils in toaster ovens use infrared waves to cook your breakfast.

Visible light The electromagnetic waves that you can see are very short—only fractions of an inch or centimeter wide. They include every single color plus white light, which is the combination of all colors. Almost half of the sunlight that reaches Earth comes as visible light.

Ultraviolet In small doses, UV rays, which also come from the Sun, can help your body produce Vitamin D, but larger doses can damage your skin and eyes.

X-rays X-rays carry a large amount of energy. They are able to go through soft substances like skin to create a picture of your bones.

Gamma rays High-energy gamma rays can penetrate all matter. They are released by the Sun, but absorbed by Earth's atmosphere before they can do any damage. Gamma rays are also released in nuclear explosions.

Cavendish Laboratory, Cambridge University, 1873

While studying the phenomena of electric and magnetic fields, Scottish-born physicist James Clerk Maxwell discovers that electricity and magnetism are linked and travel in waves equal to the speed of light. From this discovery, Maxwell deduces that light is a form of electromagnetic radiation. He also theorizes that electromagnetic waves exist at all sorts of wavelengths. This is confirmed ten years later when Heinrich Hertz discovers radio waves, which also travel at the speed of light but have much longer wavelengths than visible light.

This is a satellite map of the atmosphere over Antarctica, taken in 1992. The black and purple areas have little or no ozone.

Antarctica, 1980s

Scientists confirm that a hole the size of the United States has opened in the atmosphere over Antarctica. A smaller hole opened over the Arctic. Chemical gases called chlorofluorocarbons, or CFCs, released into the atmosphere are to blame. CFCs break down the ozone layer, which is found between 9 and 30 miles (14 and 48 km) above Earth. The layer acts as a filter for ultraviolet rays from the Sun. In large doses, ultraviolet radiation can affect the genes of plants and animals and cause skin cancer in humans.

CFCs have been banned worldwide, but some are still being released into the atmosphere from old refrigerators that are still used in developing countries. It may take centuries to reverse the damage. Punta Arenas, Chile, has times during the day when it is unsafe to go outside because of the dangerous UV rays.

A Battlefield in France, 1914

At the outbreak of World War I, Marie Curie outfits a car with X-ray equipment and travels to the front lines of battlefields to treat wounded soldiers. "Will it hurt?" asks a soldier as he sees Curie setting up her mobile lab. "No more than having your picture taken," she answers with a smile.

An early investigator of radiation and Nobel-prize winning discoverer of radium, Marie Curie answered the soldier with the best of her knowledge. X-rays were such a new discovery that no one fully understood their potential for harm. In small doses, X-rays help doctors look at broken bones and are used to treat many types of cancer. In large doses, they can actually cause some cancers. That's why today, medical personnel who take X-rays all day long stand behind lead shields—the rays cannot go through lead.

Activity

LIGHT FILES List all the ways you come in contact with the electromagnetic spectrum in a single day. Do a little research to see which seem to be the most helpful wavelengths. Then make a poster advertising all the great things they do.

HighLIGHTS
of Light Theories

About 1000 AD	1666	1690	1800-1862	1865-1873

Alhazen, an Arab scholar, contradicts the common belief that light shoots out of the eyes in order for people to see. He offers the theory that light originates in sources such as the Sun or a candle's flame, reflects off objects, then enters the eyes.

Isaac Newton (below) conducts experiments with light and color, explaining that white light is made up of all the colors in the spectrum. The British mathematician and physicist also notes that seeing certain colors is the result of some colors being absorbed by and reflected from objects. Newton's work also offers the particle theory of light: light travels as particles.

Dutch mathematician and physicist Christian Huyghens (below) publishes the theory that because light moves so quickly, it must travel in waves. This is called the wave theory of light.

Infrared is discovered as "heat" beyond the visible spectrum of light by Britain's Sir William Herschel. He finds that infrared has a wavelength longer than the red light that we normally see. By measuring light rays reflecting from a spinning mirror, French physicist Jean Bernard Leon Foucault (below) successfully calculates the speed of light.

James Clerk Maxwell (below), a Scottish scientist, discovers that visible light is a form of electro-magnetic radiation. He proposes the idea of a continuous electromagnetic spectrum.

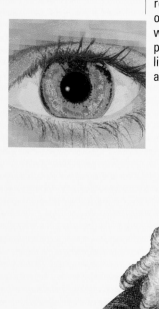

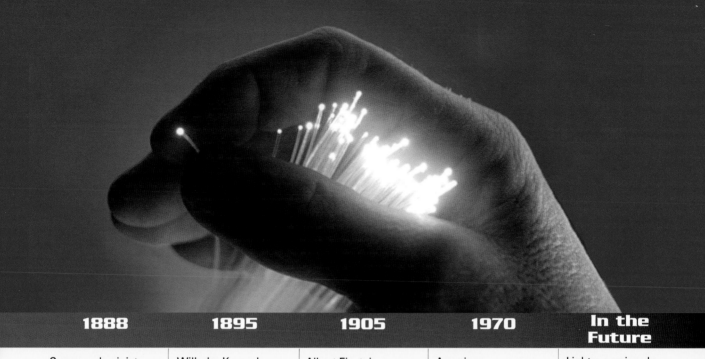

1888	1895	1905	1970	In the Future
German physicist Heinrich Hertz (below) discovers radio waves. He shows that the frequency and wavelength of electromagnetic waves can be measured.	Wilhelm Konrad Roentgen discovers X-rays, which are invisible rays with a shorter wavelength than visible light. For his discovery, the German physicist receives the first Nobel Prize for physics in 1901.	Albert Einstein describes how the immense gravity of very large objects, such as galaxies and stars, can bend light. Einstein also shows why nothing is faster than the speed of light in a vacuum and later describes how particles of light, or photons, can generate an electrical charge, known as the photoelectric effect.	American researchers at Corning Glass, Robert Maurer, Donald Keck, and Peter Schultz, perfect material to hold pulses of laser light that can carry 65,000 times more information than conventional copper wire. Their creation, made from very thin glass fibers, is called fiber optics (above).	Light as a singular power—making electronics work without electricity! That means one day, light may power entire computers, providing immediate access to information from all over the world.

Activity

SPEEDY SPACE CALCULATIONS In 1862, Leon Foucault calculated that light travels at a speed of about 186,000 miles (299, 274 km) in one second. If there are about 31.5 million seconds in a year, that means light travels about 5.859 trillion miles (9.43 trillion km) in one year! This distance is known as a light year. If it takes light from the Sun about 8 minutes to reach Earth, how far away is the Sun? How long would it take for light to reach Pluto, which lies about 3.5 billion miles (5.63 billion km) from the Sun? If the closest star, Proxima Centauri, lies 4.3 light years from Earth, how many miles (km) away is that?

11

Eye See

Around the Bend

Light bends, or refracts, when it passes from one material to another. Refraction is what makes a straw appear "broken" at the point where it passes from air into a clear liquid, and makes people appear short and stocky when they stand in a pool. Scientists rate the amount light bends in different substances as the Index of Refraction of the substance. The higher the number, the more light bends as it passes through.

Air	1.003
Water	1.33
Plastic (polystyrene)	1.49
Window Glass	1.51
Crystal	1.62
Diamond	2.42

The Great Debate

Is Light a Wave?

Holland, 1690

Christian Huygens (pronounced high jens) was a Dutch physicist who laid the foundation of wave theory of light, which explained reflection and refraction. In his book, *Treatise on Light*, he said:

"If, in addition, light takes time for its passage . . . it will follow that this movement, impressed on the intervening matter, is successive, and consequently it spreads, as sound does, by spherical surfaces and waves, for I call them waves from their resemblance to those which are seen to be formed in water when a stone is thrown into it, and which present a successive spreading as circles, though these arise from another cause, and are only on a flat surface!"

Or a Particle?

Switzerland, 1921

Albert Einstein didn't agree with Huygens' ideas on light as a wave. "[The wave theory] is not able to explain certain fundamental properties of the phenomena of light. Why is the occurrence of a certain photochemical reaction only dependent on the color, but not on the intensity of light? Why are short-wave rays in general more effective than long-wave rays? . . . The undulation theory in today's version gives no answer to these questions. . . ."

Einstein later defines the photoelectric effect. It depends on light traveling as packets of energy, called photons, to describe how light can create a current when it strikes a light-sensitive metal.

The answer? Light behaves as both a wave and a particle, but it is best understood as being composed of packets of energy called photons.

Bringing It Into Focus

When an eye doctor rates your vision as 20/20, it means that from a distance of 20 feet (6 m), the bottom line of a typical eye chart is clearly in focus, and looks to be 20 feet away. A rating of 20/40 means that at 20 feet, the chart looks to be 40 feet (12 m) away. Many people with vision above 20/40 require eyeglasses, at least for seeing distances. This means that a person with 20/200 vision would have to move up to 20 feet to see a letter a person with "perfect" 20/20 vision could see at 200 feet (61 m)! Of course, many eye charts in doctors offices are adjusted so the patient does not need to stand at 20 feet to be tested.

Need for Speed

If you could travel at the speed of light, here's how long it would take you to get to different places in the universe:

Los Angeles to New York	.0016 seconds
Around the Equator	.133 seconds
Venus	2.5 minutes
Mars	4.1 minutes
Center of the Milky Way	30,000 years
Most distant galaxy	13 to 15 billion years

Color Combos

Combining Light Colors: Red, blue, and green lights are known as the primary colors. When all three are mixed, they make white light.

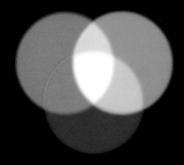

Combining Pigment Colors: When red, blue, and green pigments are combined, they have an additive effect that produces other colors. All three together make black.

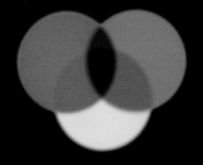

From a Distance

- Nearsighted vision means that only "near" objects are in focus. This happens if your eyeball is too long, making images focus before they hit your retina. Concave lenses (right) correct this by causing light rays to spread out, projecting the image farther back in your eye.

- Farsighted people see distant objects fine, but close-up objects may be blurry. This happens if your eyeball is too short, and images come into focus behind the retina. Convex lenses (right) help light rays come together before entering your eyes, shortening the focal length and bringing the image into focus on the retina.

Activity

ANOTHER GREAT DEBATE Now you know how to correct the vision of someone who is nearsighted or farsighted. But what if someone is both? Some people have an astigmatism that makes one eye see differently than the other. Do some research on an invention Benjamin Franklin made to correct this problem. How does his invention work? Pretend you live in the late 1700s, Franklin's time. Write him a letter explaining why his invention is helpful and suggesting another eye-related invention he could create.

More Than Meets THE EYE

Your ability to remember images, see distance, tell colors apart, and even dream, shows the ways in which the brain plays a huge role in helping you see. But how does it all work? You are about to find out.

Magically, you've just become a ray of shining white light. Eyes love you; you're very important to them. While the eyes are powerful light collectors, they must work together with a brain for vision to occur. This partnership accounts for about 60 percent of a brain's activity.

Immediately, you bounce off a distant object and race toward an opened eye.

Bending slightly and moving quick as a blink, you flash in, piercing the tough, protective cornea as you plunge toward the center. The cornea in this particular person is perfect—slightly curved, so you have no problem getting through.

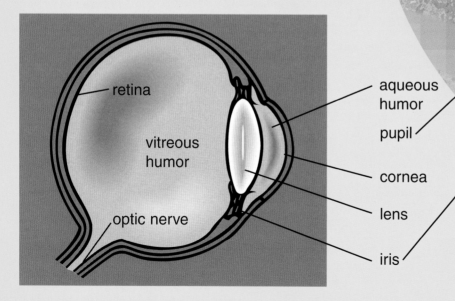

retina

vitreous humor

optic nerve

aqueous humor

pupil

cornea

lens

iris

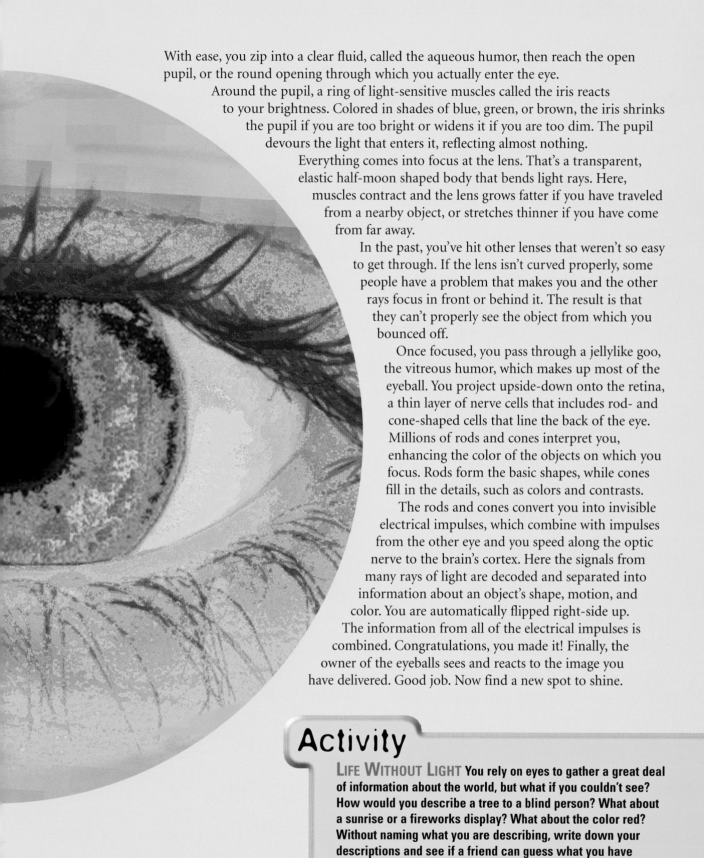

With ease, you zip into a clear fluid, called the aqueous humor, then reach the open pupil, or the round opening through which you actually enter the eye.

Around the pupil, a ring of light-sensitive muscles called the iris reacts to your brightness. Colored in shades of blue, green, or brown, the iris shrinks the pupil if you are too bright or widens it if you are too dim. The pupil devours the light that enters it, reflecting almost nothing.

Everything comes into focus at the lens. That's a transparent, elastic half-moon shaped body that bends light rays. Here, muscles contract and the lens grows fatter if you have traveled from a nearby object, or stretches thinner if you have come from far away.

In the past, you've hit other lenses that weren't so easy to get through. If the lens isn't curved properly, some people have a problem that makes you and the other rays focus in front or behind it. The result is that they can't properly see the object from which you bounced off.

Once focused, you pass through a jellylike goo, the vitreous humor, which makes up most of the eyeball. You project upside-down onto the retina, a thin layer of nerve cells that includes rod- and cone-shaped cells that line the back of the eye. Millions of rods and cones interpret you, enhancing the color of the objects on which you focus. Rods form the basic shapes, while cones fill in the details, such as colors and contrasts.

The rods and cones convert you into invisible electrical impulses, which combine with impulses from the other eye and you speed along the optic nerve to the brain's cortex. Here the signals from many rays of light are decoded and separated into information about an object's shape, motion, and color. You are automatically flipped right-side up. The information from all of the electrical impulses is combined. Congratulations, you made it! Finally, the owner of the eyeballs sees and reacts to the image you have delivered. Good job. Now find a new spot to shine.

Activity

LIFE WITHOUT LIGHT You rely on eyes to gather a great deal of information about the world, but what if you couldn't see? How would you describe a tree to a blind person? What about a sunrise or a fireworks display? What about the color red? Without naming what you are describing, write down your descriptions and see if a friend can guess what you have written about.

Seeing the Light...
and Colors

Meet a Man with a Plan

A terrifying plague is sweeping through London, killing more than 70,000 people and forcing 23-year-old Cambridge University teacher Isaac Newton to flee to the English countryside. While the university will remain closed for the next two years, Newton fills his days with experiments. Using a triangular-shaped block of glass called a prism, the young scientist investigates how this object seems to "split" white sunlight into a rainbow-colored spectrum.

In 1665, most scientists believe that light is a pure substance that cannot be broken down into smaller parts and that substances added to light make different colors. Newton's experiments, as recorded in the following excerpts from his notebook, prove those scientists wrong.

Newton experimenting with light

Notebook Excerpts:

"Having darkened my chamber and made a small hole in my window-shuts to let in a convenient quantity of the sun's light, I placed my prism at this entrance that it might be thereby refracted to the opposite wall. It was at first a very pleasing [diversion] to view the vivid and intense colors produced. . . ."

Newton keeps experimenting with the prism until he is sure that light always splits into the same spectrum of colors.

"[I] tried what would happen by transmitting light through parts of the glass of [different] thicknesses, or through holes in the window of divers bignesses, or by setting the prism without, so that the light might pass through it and be refracted before it was terminated by the hole. But I found none of those circumstances material. The fashion of the colors was in all cases, the same."

But he was only half there. When Newton passed the "split" light through a second prism, he made another discovery: the colors returned to white light.

"I took another prism like the former and so placed it that the light, passing through them both, might be refracted contrary ways, and so by the latter returned into that course from which the former had diverted it. . . . The event was that the light which by the first prism was diffused into an oblong form was by the second reduced into an orbicular one with as much regularity as when it did not pass through them."

Finally, Newton makes the conclusion that white light is made up of all the colors in the spectrum.

"Hence therefore it comes to pass that white is the usual color of light, for light is a confused aggregate of rays endued with all sorts of colors, as they are promiscuously darted from the various parts of luminous bodies. And of such a confused aggregate, as I said, is generated whiteness, if there be a due proportion of the ingredients; but if any one predominate, the light must incline to that color, as it happens in the blue flame of brimstone, the yellow flame of a candle, and the various colors of the fixed stars."

Newton sums up his experiments with an explanation of color:

"The colors of all natural bodies have no other origin than this, that they are variously qualified to reflect one sort of light in greater plenty than another."

Rainbow Bright

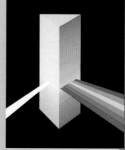

Newton discovered that as light passes through the angled edges of a prism, each color refracts by a different angle. Red light refracts by the least amount, and violet, the most. Regardless of the size of the prism or amount of light, the colors always separate into the same spectrum: red, orange, yellow, green, blue, and violet.

Why the colors of the rainbow appear in falling drops of rain is also evident from Newton's experiments. Drops that refract the rays appear purple in greatest quantity to our eye. They refract the rays of other colors so much less that they actually make them pass beside it. These other colors fill the drops on the inside of the primary bow and on the outside of the secondary or exterior one.

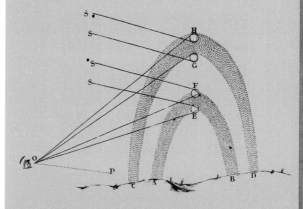

Newton's rainbow sketch illustrates how drops of water, like a prism, refract sunlight, splitting it into a rainbow, and how refraction can form a secondary rainbow underneath, with the order of the colors reversed.

Activity

DOUBLE VISION Place a prism near a closed window so that sunlight hits it. Note the colors you see. Then, take the prism outside and place it in sunlight. Do you see the same colors? Is there a difference between the two locations? What might that have to do with light waves?

Seeing Isn't Always Believing

Can you believe everything you see? Not always. While your eyes are powerful light collectors with a high-speed connection to your brain, your brain doesn't process every signal it receives correctly. Often it will take shortcuts to speed up the process of seeing, relying on past experience and visual clues that suggest what should be there. Many optical illusions occur when your brain interprets these clues incorrectly. Other types of illusions, such as a mirage or the distorted reflections in funhouse mirrors, are caused by light bending in odd ways before it reaches your eyes.

Take a look at these numbered pictures and describe what you see. Then look at the box on the right for explanations.

2 Natural Wonder

When might you see this picture in the sky?

1 Great Gaze

Are there circles in this grid?

3 Fill in the Blanks

What is this?

4 Look Out for Puddles

Can you find the water in this picture?

5 Man on Mars

Does this photo, taken on Mars, prove there's life on Mars?

6 Spiral Surprise

Does this rectangle have straight lines?

7 Double Trouble

What animal is this?

ANSWERS

❶ The contrast between dark and light is clear at the edges of the dark blocks. Yet when the lines intersect, things literally get fuzzy. At the points of each square you see gray spots, or "after images" of the darker color.

❷ Sometimes when you are in an airplane above the clouds and the light is just right, you can see an image of the airplane surrounded by a rainbow on the clouds below. This surrounding rainbow is called a glory.

❸ When you look at something familiar, your brain usually needs only a few clues to know what you are seeing. If you look closely, the dark blotches almost seem to come together. This is a man on a horse.

❹ You may think you see a pool of blue water, but you're wrong. Light rays that hit a layer of hot air near the surface of a highway or the desert bend due to the change in temperature, and reflect distant objects just above the ground's surface, creating a mirage or false image. These shimmering "puddles" on hot highways or deserts are actually reflections of the sky.

❺ This 1976 picture shows what some people thought might be proof of life on Mars. More recent pictures taken from different angles make scientists think the image is all in our brain. Shadows trigger your brain to "fill in" the familiar contours of a face.

❻ That's a perfect rectangle with four straight sides. A sense of motion and depth is suggested by this series of circles, which draws your eye into the center. This makes the rectangle's straight lines look as if they are bending inward.

❼ If you say you see a duck, you're right! But you are also right if you see a rabbit. If your eye catches the left side of the picture first, you were probably struck by a duck's bill. If you notice the right side first, your eye picked up the nose of a bunny—with its ears pulled back.

Activity

USE YOUR ILLUSION Have you ever noticed that the Moon appears larger when it sits near the horizon, and returns to "normal" when it climbs higher in the sky? Test this illusion with a coin. Observe the moon near the horizon, and hold up a coin to compare its relative size. Wait a few hours until the moon sits high in the sky, then compare its size to the coin again. What do you notice? Explain.

MAP

Bright Ideas

One of the first inventions that used light as a resource was the sundial. After noticing that a shadow was cast over the land as the sun came up and went down, Egyptians in 2000 BC were inspired to make an instrument that could tell the time of day based on the Sun's shadow. Circular slabs of stone with markings to show twelve parts of a day—two hours each—were angled on the ground to take note of the direction that the Sun's rays were falling.

Of course, sundials are useless in cloudy weather, and the sundial had to be perfectly lighted each day. But no one was discouraged. People went right on making inventions that use light and the electromagnetic spectrum as a special tool. Here are just a few bright ideas that have come from inventors and scientists around the world.

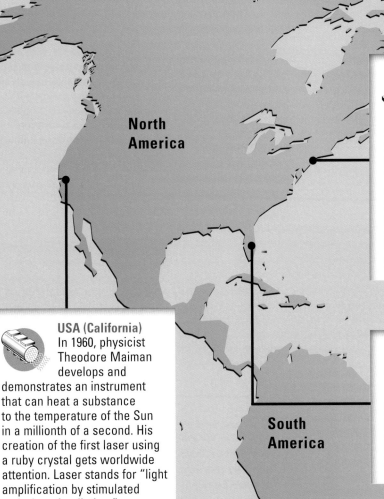

North America

South America

USA (New York)
Chester F. Carlson, a New York City attorney with a chemistry background, grows tired of constantly hand-writing copies of special documents. In 1938, he uses a process called xerography (Greek for "dry writing") to print a few words on a glass slide using light phenomena and India ink. In 1959, Xerox introduces Carlson's invention as an office copier.

USA (California)
In 1960, physicist Theodore Maiman develops and demonstrates an instrument that can heat a substance to the temperature of the Sun in a millionth of a second. His creation of the first laser using a ruby crystal gets worldwide attention. Laser stands for "light amplification by stimulated emission of radiation."

USA (Florida)
The Hubble Space telescope, designed by the National Aeronautic Space Administration (NASA) and the European Space Agency to be the most powerful observatory in space, is launched into orbit in 1990.

Scotland
Inventor John Logie Baird builds a camera that scans objects with a strong beam of light. He then becomes the first person to transmit live, recognizable moving pictures to a remote receiver. The year is 1925, and this is the start of television.

England
In response to the British Air Defense Committee's requests, Robert Watson Watt designs radar to detect aircraft in 1935. Radar, which stands for "radio detection and ranging," uses radio waves.

England
Joseph Swan invents the first electric lightbulb in 1878. The next year, Thomas Edison perfects the bulb so that it doesn't burn out after a few hours.

Holland
Hans Lippershey, a lens maker, invents the telescope in 1608. While toy telescopes are supposedly already being used in Paris, Lippershey is the first to go public with a real model. One year later, Galileo uses the telescope to study the sky and confirms that Earth rotates around the Sun.

Holland
In 1590, Hans and Zacharias Janssen mount two lenses in a tube to produce the first compound microscope. In 1672, Antoine Van Leeuwenhoek takes the idea further. He creates a microscope that magnifies things to 270 times their size. This enables him to see bacteria.

Europe

Africa

France
The motion picture camera and projector are introduced by Louis and Auguste Lumiere in 1895. Though they are the first to present the idea to a paying audience, many people argue that American Thomas Edison invented movies. Four years earlier, he created the kinetoscope, an instrument through which one person can view moving pictures.

France
Inventor Joseph Niépce produces the first photograph—of Niépce's backyard. The year is 1826, and the film has to be exposed for eight hours to make the image appear.

Activity

WORLDS APART The modern-day telescope and the Hubble Space Telescope work similarly, but they are set up differently. What might be different about them? Why do they have to be different? What must all telescopes have in common? Do some research on both structures to find out.

SHINE ON

Andrew loved to visit his cousin Mary. She was famous for her practical jokes and tricks, and he never knew when she was kidding and when she was serious. But that made being with her interesting and fun. Besides, he was as much of a practical joker and tease as she was.

Ever since they were little kids they had been involved in an ongoing competition to see who could fool whom the most. At the moment they were tied: 500 to 500. Andrew knew that Mary would keep trying to think of more and more elaborate ways to trick him. But I'm ready for her, he thought, sipping her Dad's delicious vegetable soup.

Tonight Mary seemed to be in a serious mood. She wasn't saying much. But just before dessert, she leaned over and whispered, "How would you like to get really rich, really fast?"

Andrew was so surprised he just shrugged. But later, after their parents had gone out for the evening, she asked him again. "Well, sure," he answered. After all, there was a mountain bike he was dying for, and his birthday was a long way off. "I guess so. But how?"

Mary's eyes sparkled. "I think there are diamonds hidden in that old house near Oakridge Park!"

Andrew sighed. "Not that place again! Haven't we gotten into enough trouble there?" The dilapidated old house had been vacant as long as he could remember. A few years ago, Mary had dared him to go in. They had snuck out and gotten as far as the old place's front porch before they ran away, terrified. When their folks found out, they were grounded for weeks.

"Well, this time it might be worth a little trouble," Mary replied. "Someone told me that jewel thieves stashed stolen diamonds there. It IS right near the highway—a good place for a quick getaway."

"Even if there are diamonds," Andrew said, "we couldn't keep them."

"No," Mary agreed. "But I'll bet there's a reward."

Somehow, a little while later, Andrew found himself holding their only flashlight, walking over dark sidewalks to the even darker old wreck of a house. Mary had run on ahead. Shining the flashlight on the porch, Andrew saw Mary dart inside. Carefully, he traced his own path up onto the porch with the beam of the light,

noticing the night was pitch black. No moon and no nearby streetlights.

He pushed open the door and the heavy, old-fashioned glass doorknob fell off. He stuffed it into his pocket. Inside, his flashlight beam caught Mary already at the top of the stairs. "Wait up," he said. Then her excited voice came drifting down. "I've found them! There's no light here, but it's amazing! The diamonds are lighting up the whole room up here. Come see for yourself!"

Andrew stopped. He smiled to himself. "Oh, no, you don't," he thought. Then he swung the beam around the room noticing several things:

There was a giant mirror on the opposite wall.

A long straight hallway led away from the front room. At the end of the hallway, on the right-hand wall, was a doorway.

Probably leads to the kitchen, he thought. "Come on!" Mary called again. "No, you come down here," he called. He swung the beam around to light her up as she raced downstairs. "What's going on?" she demanded.

"You've gotta see what I found in the kitchen," he said. "Down that hall. I'll stand here and shine the beam and you go look."

She looked at him, puzzled. "Well, OK," she said. She ran down the hall and into the dark kitchen. Then she came back.

"There was nothing in there," she said. "And what happened to the light? Andrew? Andrew, where are you?"

And then Mary gasped. On the opposite wall, floating in air, was a huge diamond! It threw out sparkling rays of beautiful colored light.

"There really is a diamond!" she cried. "I don't believe it!"

"You shouldn't," said Andrew. "Gotcha! That's 501 for me!"

Why did Andrew realize Mary was trying to trick him? Why didn't his beam of light reach into the kitchen?

Can you explain the diamond floating in air?

Use the clues from **Clues** the mystery, as well as these facts about light.

Light only travels in straight lines.

Some materials are a source of light themselves; others reflect or refract light.

Answers on page 32.

X Marks the Unknown

Würzberg, Germany, 1895

X-rays are invisible, electromagnetic waves that have a shorter wavelength and greater energy than visible light. They were accidentally discovered by Wilhelm Conrad Roentgen, a German physics professor. One night, Roentgen was in his lab working on experiments to see if he could make cathode rays—electricity beamed through gases in a glass tube—visible outside the cathode tube. He couldn't do it, but he did see the effects of a new kind of ray that had passed through the black cardboard box that was around the cathode tube. His student, Charles Nootangle, described what Roentgen told him had happened:

"By chance he happened to note that a little piece of paper lying on his work table was sparkling as though a single ray of bright sunshine had fallen upon it lying in the darkness. At first he thought it was merely the reflection from the electric spark, but the reflection was too bright to allow that explanation. Finally he picked up the piece of paper and, examining it, found that the reflected light was given by a letter A which had been written on the paper with a [photographic chemical] solution."

This glowing letter A, Roentgen decided, had not been caused by cathode rays because the paper was too far away. Some other rays—ones that were strong enough to pass through the cardboard case—had to be responsible. Roentgen didn't know what they were, so he called them "X-rays" thinking he'd find a better name later. Of course, the name stuck. Roentgen prepared more experiments to see what other substances could be made transparent by X-rays. He wrote about his work in a paper titled, "On a New Kind of Rays" for his university:

"We soon discover that all bodies are transparent to this agent, though in very different degrees. I proceed to give a few examples: Paper is very transparent; behind a bound book of about one thousand pages I saw the fluorescent screen light up brightly, the printer's ink offering scarcely a notable hindrance.... A single sheet of tin-foil is also scarcely perceptible; it is only after several layers have been placed over one another that their shadow is distinctly seen on the screen. Thick blocks of wood are also transparent.... A plate of aluminum about 15 millimeters [6 inches] thick, though it [weakened] the action seriously, did not cause the fluorescence to disappear entirely. Sheets of hard rubber several [inches] centimeters thick still permit the rays to pass through them.... Glass plates of equal thickness behave quite differently, according as they contain lead [flint-glass] or not; the former are much less transparent than the latter. If the hand be held between the discharge-tube and the screen, the darker shadow of the bones is seen within the slightly dark shadow-image of the hand itself.... I have observed, and in part photographed, many shadow-pictures of this kind."

Wilhelm Conrad Roentgen

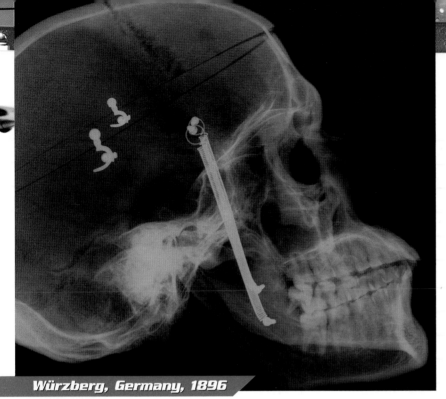

Würzberg, Germany, 1896

Roentgen's discovery soon received worldwide attention, but not all of it was favorable. Some thought photographing the skeleton of a living person was eerie and a threat to privacy. One professor told a newspaper that he couldn't sleep for a week after seeing what he called "his own death's head"—an X-ray of his skull.

Yet, for the most part, enthusiasm outweighed disapproval. *McClure's Magazine*, published in New York and London, sent reporter H. J. W. Dam to interview the scientist in his lab. Here, Dam describes meeting with the professor:

"The professor explained the mystery of the tin box. It was a device of his own for obtaining a portable dark room.

... "'Step inside,' said he, opening the door which was on the side of the box farthest from the tube.... The door was closed and the interior of the box became black darkness. The first thing I found was a wooden stool on which I resolved to sit. Then I found the shelf on the side next the tube, and then the sheet of paper prepared with barium platinocyanide. I was

thus being shown the first phenomenon ... the passage of rays, themselves wholly invisible, whose presence was only indicated by the effect they produced on a piece of sensitized photographic paper.

"A moment later, the black darkness was penetrated by the rapid snapping sound of the high-pressure current in action, and I knew that the tube outside was glowing....

"'Put the book up,' said the professor.

"I felt upon the shelf, in the darkness, a heavy book, 2 inches [5 cm] in thickness, and placed this against the plate. It made no difference. The rays flew through the metal and the book as if neither had been there, and the waves of light, rolling cloud-like over the paper, showed no change in brightness. It was a clear, material illustration of the ease with which paper and wood are penetrated. And then I laid the book and paper down, and put my eyes against the rays. All was blackness, and I neither saw nor felt anything. The discharge was in full force, and the rays were flying through my head, and for all I knew, through the side of the box behind me. But they were invisible.... Whatever the mysterious rays may be, they ... are to be judged only by their works."

Activity

TWO VIEWS Have you ever had an X-ray taken? Chances are the dentist has taken an X-ray of your mouth to detect cavities. Ask your dentist for a copy of your X-rays, and have her or him point out what each section of the X-ray shows (teeth, cavities, gums, blank space. etc.) Write a description of what you see, and explain why you think different objects are different shades of gray.

A Shining Example

Dr. Sylvia Norton uses light to help people see. Norton is an ophthalmologist, or eye doctor, who has pioneered the use of lasers in eye surgery. Her specialty is repairing the cornea—the transparent, dome-shaped structure at the front of the eyeball.

The cornea helps to focus light onto the retina at the back of the eye. Many people's eyes do not focus properly, creating blurred images. The most common focusing problem is near-sightedness. In nearsightedness, images are focused in front of the retina, and only nearby objects are seen clearly. In farsighted people, light is focused behind the retina. Sometimes light is focused on more than one spot, so that people are both near- and farsighted. This is known as astigmatism.

For years, the standard way to correct focusing problems has been to wear eyeglasses or contact lenses. In 1991, Norton was urged by the Food and Drug Administration to study a new, developing technique—a type of laser surgery called Photorefractive Keratectomy, or PRK. She was one of only 50 eye surgeons to be selected for this study. During the trial period, Dr. Norton performed laser surgery on a six-month-old baby to save him from blindness. She also experimented with the laser further, developing a technique to remove painful blisters from the cornea.

Four years later, after the PRK technique was shown to be safe and effective, it was approved for more widespread use. Today, Norton uses PRK to correct nearsightedness, farsightedness, and astigmatism.

PRK surgery involves no knives or blades. The surface of the cornea is reshaped by a cool, invisible beam of ultraviolet light from a special laser. Lasers produce intense beams of energy at a very precise wave length. Guided by a computer, Norton's laser vaporizes tiny amounts of the cornea, reshaping it to correct the focusing problem. The beam is very, very accurate. In fact, it only reshapes the outer 10 percent of the cornea. The exactness of the laser does not allow it to damage nearby tissue or even skin surrounding the eye.

Amazingly, the laser can reshape a cornea in about eighty seconds. Anesthetizing eyedrops are used, so patients feel no pain. A bandage or patch is usually placed on the eye until the surface heals. Within three to five days, most patients see an improvement in their vision. After a period of two weeks, patients are usually ready to have the second eye done.

Who comes to Norton for eye surgery? People who are uncomfortable with wearing eyeglasses or contact lenses. About 15 percent of her patients need better vision for their jobs, including pilots, police officers, race-car drivers, and people who play professional sports. After surgery, nearly all of her patients are able to drive, play sports, and watch television without glasses. In fact, Norton has joined an organization that allows her patients to donate "old" eyeglasses to people in need.

Norton practices ophthalmology in Syracuse, New York, but she has performed eye surgery and taught other surgeons in such distant places as Brazil, Portugal, and many parts of Africa. She recently started the West African Eye Foundation, which trains doctors in order to help preserve vision of people in fourteen African countries.

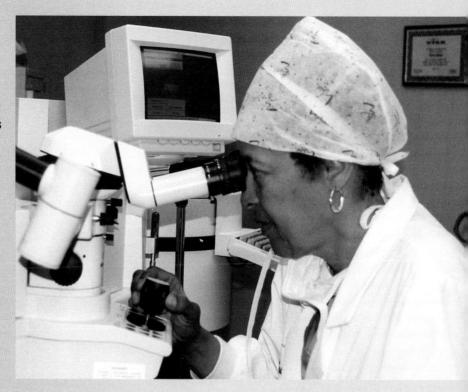

One of Norton's happiest and most rewarding experiences took place in Africa. There, she restored the vision of a ten-year-old boy who had been blind since age three—the result of a vitamin deficiency combined with a measles infection. After the successful operation, the boy's father built a special school—and named it the Sylvia Norton School for Blind Children.

"Eyesight is very, very precious," says Norton. Do all you can to protect your vision, she urges. Wear protective eye gear for sports activities, stay away from fireworks, and eat plenty of vegetables. The vitamins in them have been shown to make eyes healthier.

Norton grew up in a family of seven children. Each of her six siblings had impaired vision. Three of them were born with a hereditary eye problem that made them legally blind. "That's why at a very early age," she says, "I told my mother that I wanted to be an eye doctor." So far she has used laser surgery to help several thousand patients—and improved the lives of countless others around the world.

Activity

BE A BELIEVER Why have laser surgery? Look at the eye diagram on page 14. Notice the way the cornea curves around the pupil. Now, go back and look at the concave and convex lenses on page 13. Use your imagination to place copies of each lens in front of the eye. Now think about light rays passing through each lens. How does each lens bend the light so that it reaches the pupil? Try sketching the picture so you can understand it.

Through a Creature's Eyes

The Eyes Have It

Have you ever dreamed of being able to see behind you without turning your head? Well, if you were a bug, you wouldn't have to dream.

Humans have what are called "simple eyes." Each eye has only one lens. When light passes through the opening of the eye, it is focused by the lens on the retina. The retina has receptors that send visual information along the optic nerve to the brain.

Insects, on the other hand, have "compound eyes." A compound eye is divided into many different eyelets. An eyelet is like a mini-eye with one or more lenses. Each eyelet picks up light from a different part of the insect's surroundings. The bug's brain then takes these separate images and combines them into one. The completed image might resemble the patchwork of a quilt.

Don't even bother trying to get close to a dragonfly. While ants have about 150 eyelets and houseflies have several thousand, a dragonfly can have up to 10,000! In fact, its huge eyes take up most of its head. The thousands of eyelets allow the bug to see in front, below, and behind all at the same time.

Spot the Colors, Spot!

It looks like you can stop feeling sorry for poor old Spot and his feline pals. For years, scientists believed that dogs and cats were completely colorblind, which meant they couldn't tell colors apart. Scientists thought these animals saw colors simply as shades of gray, black, and white. Now that's changed.

Recent studies have shown that cats and dogs have two types of cells that allow them to see different colors. Cats and dogs seem to be able to see the colors blue, indigo, and violet. This means that, like 4 percent of the human male population, they are "red to green colorblind."

Knowing this, you may wonder about "seeing eye" dogs. How can they safely guide a blind person across the street if they can't tell the colors of traffic lights apart? Guide dogs learn that the position of the lights is important: when the top one lights, it means stop; when the bottom one lights, it means go.

View Master

Put yourself in someone else's eyes. Here's a flower as seen by an average human and a honey bee. Honeybees can see in ultraviolet. They are particularly attracted to yellow and blue flowers. That's because these colors have strong ultraviolet markings that make nectars easy to locate—if you are a bee, of course!

What a bee sees
(artist's rendition)

What a human sees

In the Light of Night

You're in your backyard at night. Suddenly, your flashlight shines on two glowing circles floating in the darkness! Could it be a creature from another planet looking for dinner? Not to worry. It's probably just a roaming raccoon.

The eyes of certain animals that hunt at night—such as raccoons, possums, and owls—glow when flashed with light. That's because these animals' eyes are equipped with a special feature: a thin, mirror-like membrane called the tapetum. To see how the tapetum creates the "glowing eye" effect, we have to follow light as it travels through a night creature's eye.

Animals that hunt at night usually have extra-large pupils that can open very wide. This allows more light to enter their eyes and can make things clearer in a dark environment.

Once past the animal's pupil, light travels to the eye's retina, which is connected to the brain by the optic nerve. The retina in humans is a combination of cells that help us see in bright light and cells that aid us in seeing in dim light. Since night creatures rarely encounter bright light, they tend to have few cells that help them see bright light. In fact, many bats and some snakes have none of these cells at all.

Any light that passes through the retina strikes the tapetum. The reflective material sends the light back through the retina, giving the animal's eye a second chance to pick up more of the image. Light that remains after this second pass flashes back out of the eye. This leftover light shines back at you, causing the "glowing eye" effect. Spooky!

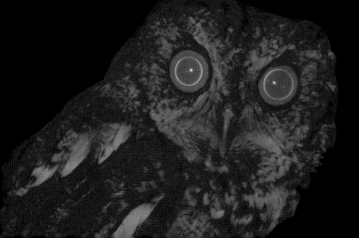

Activity

OTHER EYE-DEAS Imagine you could change your eyes into those of another creature. Which would you choose? Remember, you need to keep up your daily routine of school, sports, and so on. What would be the benefits and draw-backs of your new eyes? Write down your view of the "perfect" eye—one that combines all of the best eye "abilities" that would help you in your life. It's okay to include human eye features as well. Get creative!

Light Brights

Bouncing Beams

Mirrors aren't just for seeing your reflection. In 1969, *Apollo* astronauts placed a mirror on the Moon. Back on Earth, scientists shined a laser at the mirror and recorded how long it took for the beam to reach the Moon and reflect back: 2.6 seconds. Because they knew the speed of light, they were able to calculate the distance from one spot on Earth to one spot on our Moon as 238,857 miles (384,321 km).

Couch Potato Waves

When you press the buttons of the remote control to change channels on TV, you are stimulating a beam of infrared waves, which travel from the device in your hand to a receiver in the television, telling it to flip the channels.

Sunny Shine

In two weeks, Earth receives as much energy from the Sun—in all the wavelengths of the electromagnetic spectrum—as all the world's stored supply of coal, oil, and gas.

Brilliant Bugs

Fireflies, also known as lightning bugs, produce heatless flashes of green-yellow or red-orange light as they fly through the night sky. The little light is caused by a chemical reaction in the insect's abdomen, and it is controlled by its nervous system. While most scientists agree the light is a mating signal, some also think it attracts prey or offers a warning signal.

Optimal Optics

Beams of light bringing you information . . . imagine that! It's already the real deal. Fiber optics transmit messages by light pulses through glass or plastic fiber rods that can be as thin as hair.

Smaller and lighter than your average cable, fiber optics can send large amounts of information that result in simultaneous telephone conversations, television pictures, and computer interaction all over the world.

Fiber optics (right) are usually found in bunches. When a bundle of the fibers is arranged in the same order throughout its length, a pattern of information or an image moves through the wires. Chances are you've come in contact with the special cables. More than 80 percent of the world's long-distance telephone systems use fiber optic cable.

Sparkle Plenty

The world's largest cut diamond is the Star of Africa. It has seventy-four sides whose edges act like a large group of prisms. Light enters the diamond and splits into brilliant colors that are reflected out again in a dazzling display.

Light as Art

In the late 1800s, a new style of painting that celebrated the glory of light became popular. Impressionistic painting uses bold brush strokes to focus on the play of light and color to create an "impression" of a scene rather than a realistic image. Strokes of thicker layers of light-colored paint can make objects in a painting appear to be "lit," as in Vincent Van Gogh's Starry Night (above).

DEATH BY LIGHT

Legends says that Archimedes, a Sicilian mathematician and inventor who lived in the second century BC, used a death-ray machine on his enemies. When the Romans attacked his city, he set fire to them by creating a fire with sunlight shining through glass.

How could he really have done this? If you put two prisms together, base to base, light passes through each prism and is bent toward its base. This way, light passing through the top prism is bent down, as light going through the lower prism is bent upwards. Together, the rays of light come together at the middle. The two prisms together form a convex lens, like a magnifying glass. The point at which the light rays come together not only concentrates light into a space, but also heat. To burn the Roman fleet, Archimedes would have had to catch a whole lot of light and would have needed a gigantic magnifying glass. In other words, science shows us that Archimedes could not have actually burned the Roman enemies.

Doorknob Head

A condition called doorknob head affects every single person. When you look into a brass or silver doorknob, you will find your face is out of shape: maybe your chin is bigger than the rest of your head, or your eyes are spread far apart.

This happens because a doorknob has a curved surface, so the rays of light that bounce into it reflect in odd ways, producing a distorted image. The wacky mirrors in fun houses or amusement parks work the same way.

Whiter Whites

Some laundry detergents contain phosphors, which absorb the invisible ultraviolet light in sunlight. The ultraviolet light causes the phosphors to glow in visible light, making whites look whiter and bright colors look brighter.

Let's imagine you can't communicate by sound—a problem in space. You may try to use light because it travels at a constant, speedy rate. In fact, if you could bounce a light beam between a mirror in New York and a mirror in Los Angeles, it would make thirty round trips in a second!

Now you've just been hired to be a part of a team of engineers. Your challenge is to create a model to illustrate how light waves can be used for communication. In truth, a flashlight wouldn't be the best way to communicate in space, but you are simply creating a model. This model needs to meet the following criteria:

- Uses at least two types of mirrors or lenses—flat, concave, or convex

- Can send a light wave around at least two corners

- Can send a light wave up or down (i.e. ceiling to floor)

- Includes a code to understand a message

- Uses a flashlight as the source of the light

- Can be used with young children to help them understand light as a wave

Here's what you need to do:

1. In groups of three or four, research how different lenses redirect light waves.

2. Obtain a variety of mirrors and lenses. Explore what you learned from research by shining light from the flashlight on each. Set up combinations of these lenses and mirrors to help you decide which ones to use.

3. Create your code. Practice sending and decoding messages with your team.

4. Write an explanation of your mirror/lens arrangement that you can give fellow classmates following your demonstration. Be sure to include illustrations and examples.

5. How has the need to communicate in space improved our methods for communicating here on Earth? Present your model to the class and include the answer to this question in a short speech.

6. For a real challenge, think about how we can use other forms of light from the electromagnetic spectrum to communicate.

ANSWERS
Solve-It-Yourself Mystery, pages 22–23:

1. Diamonds reflect light; they don't glow. In a completely dark house, Mary would not have seen diamonds sparkling.

2. The beam of light could not go down a hallway and turn a corner into the kitchen.

3. Andrew shined his flashlight on the cutglass doorknob, sending its reflection into the mirror across the room. The doorknob acted as a prism, splitting light into different colors—like a diamond would.